THAT LOOKS GREAT!!!

Simple

Artistic

FOOD PRESENTATION

AMERY WARE

To order additional copies of this book, contact:
Xlibris
1-888-795-4274
www.Xlibris.com
Orders@Xlibris.com

ISBN: 978-1-7960-5759-1 (sc)
ISBN: 978-1-7960-5760-7 (hc)
ISBN: 978-1-7960-5758-4 (e)

Library of Congress Control Number: 2019913870

Print information available on the last page

Rev. date: 09/19/2019

CONTENTS

"THAT LOOKS GREAT!"

SIMPLE ARTISTIC FOOD PRESENTATION

ABOUT THE AUTHOR

I've been an artist of some kind or another my entire life. From my early days in NY, I starting with writing songs and rhymes in school, and moved on to writing graffiti on walls. Then I was breaking and dancing, spending countless nights exploring Manhattan nightclubs and the artsy scene. I can tell you that during the late 80s to early 90s, I was deeply involved in or somehow close to the action in the beginning of the "**New Jack Swing**" music movement. I lived in the same small town of **Mount Vernon**, NY where many music and entertainment people came from.

My moms' house was a few blocks away from the home where **Art Carney**, who played **Ed Norton** on the original **Honeymooners** TV sitcom grew up. **Denzel Washington** also grew up and started **The Boys and Girls Club of America** in my hometown. **R&B** singing sensation, **Al B.Sure!** and the late rapper **Heavy D** were good friends of mine and they also lived a stone's throw away from where I did.

To be honest, there are too many names of important people from the sports or entertainment industry to list and stay on the subject of this book, so I'll move on. I can tell you if you ever get the chance to visit my old high school, **Mt. Vernon High School** on **California Road** in **Westchester NY**, there is a hallway that has a Wall of Fame with pictures of most of the people who came from and or grew up there. It was a place that seemed like everybody was doing something artistic. If I wasn't part of the movement directly, I was always somewhere around it.

I was there when **Andre Harrell** started **Uptown Records** in a little spot in Brooklyn. I even helped move some of the furniture in! I was there when **Russell Simmons** taped the 1st episode of **Def Comedy Jam**. If you get to see any of the original episodes and see the intro when **Kid Capri** announces the show, it was Russell, myself and a few other close friends of mine running into the building when they did the opening to the show.

I was there, at a place called the **Skate Key Roller Rink** on **Allerton Avenue** in the **Bronx**, when **Doug E. Fresh and Slick Rick** performed the live version of the song "**La Di Da Di**" before it was even recorded as the record that made them a hit group. Being around all that, eventually led to the formation of my own music group called **F.S. Effect!** and a short stint in the music industry. I did earn a platinum plaque for the solo performance that I was blessed to have included on one of the top selling movie soundtracks to date, "**New Jack City**", which was produced by **Al B. Sure!**

I was there when four guys from down south arrived in NY, with their **GOD** given talent and determination to fulfill their dreams of becoming recording artists. I got to see them become the multi platinum **R&B** group, **Jodeci**.

I was even blessed enough to have them provide vocals on a few of my own groups' records before they came out with their own. I also convinced one of my favorite rappers at the time, **Prince Markie Dee** from the legendary group, **The Fat Boys** who had not rapped on a record since the breakup of his group, to grace us with his presence and do a verse on a song from my own album. I was the one who personally picked a young dancer named **Josie Harris**, out of a line up of girls auditioning to be in my first

music video. It was also her first real TV dance gig but she went on from there to be one of the hottest "**Fly Girls**", a group of dancers on the show, **In Living Color** even before **Jennifer Lopez** got her start as a dancer on the same show.

My point is that I've been around. I've been blessed to see and do some things most people only dream about.

As time went on, I was still looking to expand my creative horizons. I was getting older, watching times change around me and I wanted to explore other ways to express my creativity. I was thinking of the best way for me to show the world my artistic viewpoint in other ways after my music career. I was looking for still more lucrative ways to be productive while possessing the freedom to display my imagination. Finally I decided, what better way than cooking!

I went to the **NY Restaurant School,** located in **Manhattan** on **34th Street**, right next door to the **Empire State Building**. They offered a night school program, and I was able to go to school from 11pm to 7am and still work in the daytime. It was quite an experience, and during my tenure there, the school had decided to move to a larger location at **75 Varick Street**. The night school students had the honor of packing up most of the tools and equipment we used in our school kitchen, then unpacking and setting back up when we moved downtown to the new building.

I loved that the school moved to that particular building, since it was located right down the street from **S.O.B's** nightclub where my good friend **Leroy Evans**, or "**Big L**" as we called him, was the bouncer/asst club manager.

He had the say so at the door of the place and I took full advantage of it, going to the club every chance I got. Being that I spent a lot of time in that area anyway, I was familiar with the hustle and grind of the big city and it was a comfortable transition from music and dancing to cooking.

The course I took was a year long, with 6 months in school and 6 months doing an externship, or "out of the class" work at some participating restaurant. It was my externship that really changed the course of my career path. Up until that point, I still wasn't sure if the "art" thing that I was looking for would be TRULY found working with food. I did my externship in **Montclair, NJ** at a little four star restaurant tucked away in a quiet corner of that quaint and quiet town called **YVES**.

The place only had about 12 tables and was by reservation only. We used to take the reservations off the answering machine and it would always be some doctors or lawyers, mostly prestigious people with money since it was quite costly to eat there.

The chef owner was a black man named **Patrick Pierre Yves Jerome**. **Art Culinaire** magazine recognized him as one of the top black chefs in America, specializing in classic French cuisine that he put his own twists on. Man, He was great!!

I soon came to realize I wasn't totally committed to cooking until after I spent time working at **Yves**'.

Pierre played it like a true artist too. Just like a painter about to pour his heart out on to the canvas, he would show up at the kitchen about noon every day. He had his white chef coat with what looked like captains trim on the sleeves and the collar and his name in gold script, hanging by the stairs that led downstairs from the ground floor of the restaurant into the kitchen. He would literally run in, bubbling over with some new ideas for a dish, grab the coat and switch whatever he had on for that like the old children's TV show actor **Mr. Rogers**, but much more hyped up! The whole time he'd be talking to his Sous chefs and myself about what he had on his mind for that night's menu.

Oh Yes, he would come up with a new dish and the perfect presentation for it on the spot and direct us on how to make it happen. After dinner was served and the patrons satisfied, he would speak to the people at each table as they dined then casually come down stairs, take off that coat and say goodnight to us and that would be it till the next day.

The man had the magic touch when it came to food. Everything he made was fantastic! He had me eating things I never thought I'd like and even some things that I never liked, I loved when he made them. He could really throw down and he always used to say, " I don't know how to do, blank, but I can cook!" That was his little joke. Anything he didn't know or couldn't do he'd just fill in the blank of that sentence and with a big smile, let out a jolly laugh like **Santa Claus**.

I learned a lot about cooking from Pierre. I learned about how to make things taste their best through proper preparation and unique cooking methods. I learned about experimenting with different ingredients. I even learned some recipes to this day, I still have yet to encounter anyone who can make them or even know about them for that matter. But the most important thing I learned at **Yves**' was the thing that inspired this book. I learned how to **DISPLAY** food as art.

I'm not going to say my way of doing things as far as cooking goes is the BEST way, or even the most effective way. It's definitely not the only way, but I can proudly say it's always a lovely artistic way. I learned to create an artistic vision with pretty much every dish I prepared. Some dishes might even be quite basic, like macaroni and cheese for instance, but with a few additions, I learned how to make it look like something much more desirable. After I left **Yves**, I worked at a lot of different places in almost every area of the food service industry. I was a produce clerk for the old **Pathmark** supermarket chain first. That really helped to increase my knowledge of different vegetables, their freshness and the best seasonal selection times. After that, I moved on from just working around food to really cooking professionally.

If I remember correctly, my first real cooking job was for a chain **Tex Mex** restaurant called **Jose Tejas** in **Paramus, NJ**. I really enjoyed working there. They had a real wood grill to do

5

most of the food there, and every morning, the staff would come in and add large pieces of wood to the indoor grill and stoke up the fire. I learned some very interesting sauce recipes that I never tasted before working at that spot. They had their sauces brought in from an off site factory in bags, so they were all ready prepared when we would combine them with a dish during service, but I'm always looking to replicate a taste that I like and I would mentally pick it apart to reconstruct it later at home.

You see, before I was an artist or cook when I was in my pre teen years, I wanted to be a scientist. I've always been fascinated with formulas and how things work and blend together, so I guess getting into cooking was like a no brainer. I can taste something maybe once or just a few times and I can replicate the same taste or come very close to it. There are still some **Jose Tejas** restaurants around and it would become one of my favorite places to eat, but that one closed due to fire.

After that, I certified to work at **TGI Fridays** as a Saute cook. I don't know how they do it now, but back then we had to take a class for a few weeks, regardless of your prior experience to be qualified to cook at Fridays. The one I worked at was in **Woodbridge, NJ** and it was a brand new store when I started there. We were the 1st staff to take the plastic off the equipment and set up the kitchen.

It was a 5 million dollar a year location, and on weekends we had at least 6 bartenders on duty. We did no less than 1000 covers on the weekends, just Sat and Sun. This is where I learned speed and how to work in a kitchen under extreme pressure.

I remember we used to get orders behind the line on a little ticker tape computer and I tell you, when we were at peak service time, that thing **NEVER** stopped ticking. I really used to have nightmares about that and I could hear that machine ticking off orders in my sleep. On the line, the cooks would gear up like we were going to war. We would tie on bandanas and aprons just waiting for the expeditor to start calling out orders. When we opened for that nights' service, he would call out the tables as people came in and were seated. It would start, "5 open menus!", meaning that 5 people had been seated and were looking over their menus. Ten minutes later he would yell out, "27 open menus!" Ten minutes after that, " 56 open menus!" and that's how it would go on all night.

We had 7 minute appetizer times, meaning you had 7 minutes to prepare that item and have it in the window for the server, and 12 minutes for entrees, and believe me, they would be on you to keep those quotas! I worked in front of a stove that had 8 burners or "eyes" on it, and at any given time I had saute skillets going on all of them. We never left the stove while we were in service. They had a bin underneath the stove area to throw in the dirty pans and someone was always running down the line to grab your dirty ones and restock you with clean pans so you never had to leave your station during service.

We had refrigeration built in under the stoves that had everything portioned and day dotted in little bags. We had ladles numbered for every sauce we used and everything was totally portion controlled. It was quite normal that you could work an 8 hr. shift and never leave that station the whole time you were there except for an occasional smoke or bathroom break if someone could cover you.

TGI Fridays had an extremely wide variety of items you could order back then and the menu was like 15 pages, but since then they have cut down the list of items available. I think they figured out something when they introduced the **Jack Daniels** and **Whiskey** sauce recipe.

During the times I worked these jobs, I started my own catering business on the side called, **Supreme Tastes International Catering**. I still own it now but really just as a novelty since these days I don't have much time to run it being committed to a full-time job that occupies most of my time. Plus finding and keeping good, dependable people to work for you when you have your own little business is really rough.

I remember when I did my first catering job, a guy I hired took his pay as soon as we were done that night and drove off to another state! To this day I never saw him again and he left me with the task of cleaning and putting away all the equipment we used by myself! It's still funny when I think about that now.

I also worked for a few country clubs. One called **The New York Athletic Club,** had two locations. One in **Manhattan** and the other uptown near where I lived, was a resort location in **Pelham, NY**. I worked at both places. I worked at the **Pelham Country Club** and when I started moving around the U.S., I worked at **Avila Country Club** in **Tampa**, Florida. In 2003 when my daughter was born, I decided to work in the healthcare sector of the foodservice industry since usually in the restaurant business, you don't really have good options for health benefits and the hours are much more steady working in these kind of large institutions. I didn't want to work anymore late nights that would keep me away from making sure she had an active and PRESENT father in her life growing up. I worked from nursing homes to assisted living facilities and finally ended up running a hospital kitchen that prepares the food for the patients as well as providing a retail café for staff and visitors. We also do a great deal of off site catering and that's where I have been for the last ten years of my culinary career. Fortunately for me, it has been working here that allowed me the time and freedom to create most of the ideas and dishes that provide the subject matter and photos for this book. You might think it would have come from working at some fancy restaurants with large scale recognition but this book is proof for me, it isn't where your from it's where your at!

Still throughout my culinary career, I've worked for a bunch of private restaurants, all specializing in different cuisines that I was interested in exploring. I was even willing to work for no money at some places, just to get the real recipes and true grasp of the culture of the different nationalities at those places. For example, I would go into a **Chinese** or **Latin** restaurant, and ask if they needed help for the day and work for free just so I could see how they did "their thing". I didn't want to learn a **Chinese** recipe from a cook book, I wanted to work side by side with a person of that culture to learn than cuisine. I wanted to see it first hand.

My mom was born in **Jamaica**, so I got a lot of knowledge on how to make certain **Jamaican** dishes from her. She taught me how to prepare many West Indian recipes at home before

I ever started cooking professionally. **Curry Chicken, Jerk Chicken, and Rice and Peas** were staples in my house and were some of the first dishes I learned how to make.

I lived close to a place in the **Bronx** that "specialized" in **Jerk Chicken**. Descendants of The **Arawak Indians** from **Jamaica** ran this place and that's all they sold. I walked in and offered my service for a day, just so I could learn that recipe and how they did it. All the places I worked, helped to increase my skills and knowledge in the field of cooking and I desire to just give those reading this book an understanding of the scope of my experience. I hope you will enjoy my presentation as much as I enjoy serving it to you!

INTRODUCTION

When you prepare a meal for family or maybe for a festive event or special occasion, how do you see it? Do you look at it as you are feeding people some good food and you hope it's healthy and enjoyable to everyone's taste? Well of course! But is that all? Of course not. You want your food to look great as well. The better it looks, the better its GOTTA taste right? Well maybe, but one thing is for sure, if it looks good, people will truly enjoy the opportunity to eat it.

Maybe you don't have the "eye" for proper food presentation. Or maybe you don't understand the culinary importance of putting just the right amount of sauce on a stuffed chicken breast. And maybe you don't have a good handle on how not to "crowd" a plate or platter with things people don't really care to see when they're thinking about eating. Maybe, you're just used to throwing things together. You flood your dishes with sauce or serve baked items that **SHOULD** be golden brown, **WITHOUT** that finalizing touch.

Overall, you continue to find yourself falling short of the number one goal of food presentation, to give the diner that "**love at first sight**" deliverance of your food. For these reasons, the goal of this book is to show you how to present all your dishes, even the simplest ones in the best, most artistic way possible. Now you can be sure even if it's not "**Pit master**" award-winning **BBQ**, or a dish that was made by a celebrated chef, it will look like it is every time.

The freshness of the main ingredient and its proper cooking time, are of the utmost importance to ensure positive results in the presentation of the final dish. After that, there are many other components and procedures that can be added and performed to enhance the finished dish, distinguishing it from being "**nice-looking food**" to a creation that can be called a "**work of art**". These can come from fancy knife cuts or carvings. Garnishes of all types, can add vibrant color and life, and even serve to create or set a scene.

In this book I will show you many pictures of dishes I've made and how I presented them as well as tips on garnishes, carvings and other accents that will help you to make more artistic creations with your dishes. I have not included any recipes in this book because I feel **EVERYONE** has their own "**best**" recipe in their mind. If you cook, you most likely already have "**your**" way of cooking your food the way you like it, so this is not about teaching you how to make food, but more about making the food you'll make, **LOOK BETTER**.

When you hear people say, **THAT LOOKS GREAT!** and they're talking about **YOUR** dishes, you're already halfway there to having successfully created an extraordinary dining experience.

Chapter One
" F.A.M. Focus, Attitude and Mood"

Someone I worked with in the kitchen told me once that she thought I cook better when I was mad or upset about something. In reality, it wasn't that I cooked better when I was mad, but when I was mad, I would just become much more intensely focused on doing what it was that I happened to be doing at that time, which just happened to be preparing food! The added focus obviously showed in my finished products. And it wasn't that being angry made me cook better, but my mood while I was upset, triggered some extra concentration. Almost like a fighter that suddenly becomes more intense and focused after taking a good shot from his opponent. The change in mood causes a noticeable change in attentiveness.

My point is that situations that put you in certain moods or frames of mind, definitely affect how you will perform at any given time. This can be evident in many aspects of things you do in your life, even while doing something as simple as cooking.

It's obvious that a festive mood will usually allow a persons' creative juices to flow freely, but sometimes, depending on the circumstances, a less than joyous mood could have similar effects. I'm by no means trying to say you should get angry, or that you need to be mad to get stuff done, but sometimes, when you are not happy or playing around you can benefit from the seriousness of your mood.

How a person might dress while they work or create can have some impact on how their product turns out as well. If you cook in a professional capacity, it would be mandatory to wear the proper attire for working in a professional kitchen. At home or outside of this environment, a person might feel more comfortable in a Tee-shirt, shorts and some slides and still be able to make a professional effort and a wonderful product. You don't have to have on a chef hat to be a good chef but for some people to wear one, gives them that energy and push to their actions, just because of how it looks, what it represents and the way they feel when they put it on.

There are no pictures in this chapter to illustrate my points here because F.A.M. is about feelings. The way a person feels plays a major part in their actions when it comes to doing **ANYTHING**.

It's important to feel well to perform well or create well, but even if you don't feel that great or don't have that jovial mood all the time you can still focus it into a positive output when it comes to your food preparation and presentation. Understand, things might not always be in order but being in order is everything. Certain things naturally blend and go with other things.

Certain colors just "fit" with other colors. A chaotic mood does not mean you can't maintain order but what you might be trying to put in order will be that much more difficult to achieve if you don't have a clear, even state of mental steadiness. I've worked with people who are very good workers in general. Regardless of the mood they're in when they show up for work, because of their order and work routine, they are usually able to finish the task they have before them on a daily basis.

The only difference between having a good mood and a clear state of mind, and having a bad mood in regards to a workday is the flow of how things are getting done. A person in a bad mood or unclear mind state can find that many things go wrong on the way to finishing a task. A lot of unnecessary pitfalls and problems arise one after the next when a person is not in control of their emotions or are unable to control their mood. Things you would usually show a great deal of care for, become less important and they will display a noticeable lack of attention to detail. You find yourself doing things you would not usually do and even if you make it through the task successfully, you will not have the same sense of satisfaction upon its' completion that you would if you were in a good mood and working with a clear head. The point I'm trying to make is that most projects come out a lot better when the "**F.A.M**" is in order.

Chapter Two
"Stuff"

The first "things" you need to make your food look beautiful might sound like I'm trying to make you into a hoarder, but most times the more of it you have, the better off you will be. In order to create, craft and design the food you prepare into wonderful, artistic presentations you will need "**STUFF**".

"**Stuff**" is all of the things that you can use to form, shape, design and enhance how your dishes look.

"**Stuff**" will be your tools. Pots, pans, and bowls are not always used just for the purpose they were intended like just cooking or mixing in. Some of these might be used to actually "**display**" the food **after** it has been cooked. An example of this might be a small, nicely painted porcelain crockpot used solely to present a dish after it is removed from the initial pot or pan it was prepared in. Bowls can also be used for molds or maybe even be put upside down in the center of a plate to give height to a food item that may be displayed on top of it. Food placed around it on a platter would serve to hide the bowl from sight just emphasizing the item that would be placed on top of it for additional height.

Some wire and **some string** can be useful to hold certain items together in a display. **Cookie cutters** of all shapes and sizes can be used to make great designs and cuts. A lot of chefs use **PVC pipe** that you would find in a hardware store to do plumbing work and cut it into different sized rounds. These can then be used to shape and mold food items on a plate. Like you can put some rice into the **PVC cut tubing** and then pull off the tubing and the rice will hold that shape on a plate.

The same kind of molding can be done with a small cup or bowl. **Squeeze bottles, toothpicks, tape, wooden and metal skewers,** even the **lids from jars** can be used to form perfect different size burgers patties. **Knives, foil pans, parchment paper, food processors, blenders, grinders, juicers, etc. etc**. I could go on and on. If you want to turn your food into art, you do need more than just the food itself. You need "**Stuff**".

Garden items make for great stuff for plate design and presentation. **Flowers and herbs of all kinds**, some are even edible can turn a plain platter into something wonderful in seconds. You can decorate a plate with **grape vines** or a **few sprigs of thyme**. Platters with **pine cones** or **acorns** can take on the lovely appearance of a seasonal day in the fall. **Powdered sugar** or **coarse salt** can make for a great winter presentation. The possibilities are endless and most of this stuff costs little or nothing to acquire. It's a good idea to try and increase your skill with a knife and learning some carving knowledge can be a great asset to your design possibilities. Some of the garden items you might usually throw away can be turned into fabulous garnishes with just a few simple cuts if you know how to do it.

There are many schools you can go to and even ways to learn online how to carve sculptures out of melons or make garnishes from various food items, but you will still need the some tools to do this. I have been blessed to teach myself how to do many of these things on my own without spending much money for this knowledge. I have however spent some money, but not a lot mind you, acquiring "**Stuff**". All well worth the cost.

Like I said previously, many of the things you might use to artistically present food will cost little to nothing as far as real expense but in order to do some of these things professionally, you might want to invest in a few tools. A carving knife from **Thailand** was one of my first "**stuff**" items as far as tools. I wanted to learn how to carve fruits and melons, and even though I was never trained professionally, I got pretty good at it once I got the right tool to start. I watched experts from around the world carving with this special kind of knife and I was able to apply my own skill set to the use of this marvelous tool.

I found out that **large plastic storage bins with covers** counted as some good "**stuff**". I had to prepare four 25 lb. turkeys for frying. It's REALLY hard to season and marinate even ONE turkey if you don't have something to put it in! Plus I had no refrigerator space to hold these birds! Good thing I had to do this for **Christmas**. There was snow outside and the temp was pretty low so I was able to clean, season and store ALL my birds out in my backyard overnight. It might seem extreme to some but just think about what people had to do to store and preserve food before they had the modern equipment to do it, and that'll make you feel better!

Just for a quick note, turkeys that are brined and/or seasoned in large bins obviously can't be stored in any kind of home type fridge or freezer. This makes this application not all that practical for someone who doesnt have access to a large walk-in refrigerator. As I mentioned previously, there are options but I wouldn't suggest even attempting preparation of such large birds in a home setting unless you were not planning to hold them that long before cooking them. A few hours in brine at the most and maybe the same with dry rub seasoning. Other than that I suggest you leave this job to experts with the proper equipment and facilities.

I remember when I cooked the food for a **Filipino** wedding, my 1st catering function when I started out and I needed to prepare a 40 lb whole pig and 75 lbs of ribs as the main meat courses. The thing was, it was myself alone making ALL the food. I don't know if you've even worked with that much meat, but if you haven't, it's hard to work with if you don't have the proper "**stuff**", and I didn't!

I had to get a big folding picnic table to put my pig on to clean and prepare it for the grill, which I also had to make! I remind you, I didn't live in the country. I was at my mothers' house in the suburbs and it looked real crazy for the people driving down the street to see me standing in the front yard with a hose, washing a whole butchered 40 lb pig.

As for my grill, I was lucky enough to have a small backyard. I dug a pit in the ground, went to home depot and bought some heavy gauge metal grates. I'll never forget how I had to stay up most of the night and fight to keep the raccoons away from that meat! The whole neighborhood smelled like pork! But that was just another example of the importance of having the right "stuff" to do the jobs you need to do.

"**Stuff**" is not always just considered to be equipment or tools you might use. "**Stuff**" can also be other food items that you might use to enhance the presentation of the main dish you will serve. Things you might throw away like **vegetable trimmings, fruit peels, banana skins, the top you cut off the pineapple with the pointy leaves**. That's "**stuff**" too. Some **large, crusty rolls** that you can hollow out and use as bowls for the food that you might otherwise just put into a regular old bowl and serve would be considered "**stuff**". Just the presentation alone can make a little chili or stew into an exotic dish you and your guests will love to look at!

So don't throw away that pineapple top or shavings from those carrots you just peeled! They could be just the **stuff** you need to add that extra touch to your finished dishes that will make people visually desire your food and mentally believe it must be great, before they even taste anything.

I try not to waste anything if it can be used. Funny how that would translate into many different ways to bring beauty and life to otherwise simply prepared food! Another example of a food item that can be considered "**stuff**" that you will find fantastic to use as garnish are lettuce leaves. I will talk more about them and show many illustrations of their use in the next chapters since they are one of the easiest items to use as a garnish and for staging a finished dish. Once again I tell you, many items you might not think of can be used as very important "**stuff**" to help you create a lovely presentation, so use your imagination and you'll fine!

Chapter Three

" **Staging** "

The next thing I will discuss is the "**staging**". This is the most important chapter in this book since it will explain the various techniques and methods of the actual presentation of your dishes' end result. I will also provide many photos in this chapter as I have taken pictures of plenty of different examples for you.

Now, the "**stage**" is the platform you will display your food on and staging is the way it will be set up. Certain objects or parts of the food itself might be used to add height or make the food take on a creative look usually composed of components that might not be eaten as part of the dish.

Another staging example is you can slice meats on a slicing machine for setting up a cold cuts platter and make a huge difference in the appearance of your platter by folding the slices of meat and stacking them on each other in various patterns to create a fabulous look of height instead of just laying the meat on the tray, regardless of how neat you might arrange the pieces.

The smallest detail can make a huge impact on food you serve. I've used those **little paper serving trays** or I like to call them, **"boats"** you find in places that might serve "**grab and go**" type items like **chicken fingers** and **fries**. Since I only had the small boat container by itself, I would "**stack**" the food items that I wanted to present.

I served a small **chicken and waffles** platter this way by starting with one section of a large **Belgium waffle**, since a waffle maker automatically presses the waffle to be separated into four equal pieces. I was able to make four small boat platters. I was able to put the **waffle section, two chicken fingers** and **a small pc container of maple syrup** all together in the same small paper boat. It was more convenient than putting the items on a large plate, and also gave a "cute" look to the platter that attracts the eye.

People like to feel that they can get all they want in one place as quickly as possible, so having all items in the paper boat including the syrup, which at most places a person might have to acquire from another area in the restaurant, after getting there food is seen as an added time consuming problem. Nowadays at large chain restaurants like **Burger King** or **McDonald's** these holders are designed by the company specifically for items that are usually served on the side so they can be served together with the main food item as a whole meal instead of separately.

This presentation in itself, gives the food items being presented a completely different appeal to the consumer. Some places that serve **fried chicken** for instance have containers designed with different little compartments for each item provided in a meal. One part for the **chicken**, then a space that is set aside for the **fries**, and then a round compartment for a **condiment cup**, all in the same box. This looks much better than if all the food items were to be put together in a box and served with no **separation**.

Staging of dishes is limited only to the imagination of the person putting together the presentation. Color has a lot to do with staging dishes also as I will explain in the next chapter, but you can pretty much get away with many different variations of colors and settings if you are creative and have an eye for detail. As I mentioned previously, lettuce leaves are a main component in the art of food staging.

You can make food look so much better in so many different ways with just a few pieces you might not have used on your salad. **Lettuce leaves** bring a whole different **dimension of viewing** to a dish, making a main food item look like it is part of the plant itself and that its still "**growing**", yet to be picked. The limits are really your imagination. You can make a dish that you serve much more appealing and if you cater or plan to sell your food, you can actually increase your price by added some **lettuce leaves** to the display, making it even appear to be worth more than if you just served the dish by itself.

For example, take **shrimp**. Everybody who enjoys seafood usually find shrimp quite irresistible. You can boil it, roast it up, fry it and even serve it cold as a cocktail and just pile it on a platter and your guests will be sure to make it disappear for you. But if you take four or more **nice, green lettuce leaves**, and arrange them on your platter first, then pile the **cocktail shrimp** in the middle of them and add a **few lemon half moons** and **a sprinkle of fresh chopped parsley** and you will have a work of art that you can actually charge a higher price for. I have used **lettuce leaves** to stage many dishes I make and they always make it look that much more enticing.

A lot of items from the chapter on "stuff" can also be used for staging the final presentation of your dishes. **Paper** is a great staging tool since its consistency will allow you to shape it to do many things that will help you to create and finalize your carvings or platters. **Plain typing**

paper can be used as template you can tape to a melon so you can draw what you might like to carve onto your sculpture, and edit as you wish before you actually do any cutting. **Parchment paper** can be **used to add height** to a food item that you wish to highlight in your display since you can mold it and use it as a "**seat**" for the item to be featured or used as an accent on your platter. **Parchment paper** is also safe to use in contact with food items because it is **food grade** and has **no dyes or chemicals** that will affect the taste of your dish, or make it unhealthy for consumption. You can also use different compenents of the food you are serving to stage itself. Like a sauce, for instance. Many chefs will ladle sauce onto a plate before putting the food on top of the sauce. This not only makes sure you don't drown the food or over sauce the the dish but it makes a lovely presentation by providing a color background that compliments the plate. You can always serve the final dish with a bowl or container of the sauce on the side if more might be requested.

Food items can be "**stacked**" on top of itself **to achieve height** and make the dish look more pleasing to the eye. I made an **Italian** themed meal and I served the main course with **Parmesan bread sticks**. I also made a **Parm cheese sauce** for dipping the breadsticks. Instead of putting the breadsticks on the platter and serving a bowl of sauce with it, I "stacked" the breadsticks on top of each other like a **Jenga** game tower. Then I served them on a platter with the sauce underneath it. I added **a few sprigs of rosemary** and changed a very simple side dish into a wonderful work of art. It took no extra ingredients, and very little extra time.

I did the same type of staging with a **fried fish platter**. Usually the fish would be put on the platter and served with some **lemon wedges** on top or on the side of the dish. Instead I arranged **lemon and lime half moons on the platter first**, then I stacked the fish on top of the garnish itself. This way of staging a simple fried fish platter changed the look of my final presentation totally. The only thing I needed to do after that was to provide some more lemon half moons on the side for those who wanted a nice squeeze of citrus on their fish since the garnish under the food would not be reachable without destroying the whole platter.

Parchment paper is used here for the "staging" of a bowl on a appetizer platter. Start by gathering the right amount of paper you will use.

The next step will be to shape the paper into form for the right height that you need for the bowl seat.

Next you will press the empty bowl into the paper seat to create the mold that will hold the bowl in place. the reason parchment paper is great for this is that is will keep the shape because of it's consistency. When you remove the empty bowl, it will be easy to place the paper nest where you need it to be on your platter.

Place the paper nest on your empty platter first, then arrange the food items around the nest.

Add your bowl to the paper nest seat which will be slighty elevated above the food dipping items.

Add the sauce or condiment to the bowl and its done!

Staging plays a huge part in the successful presentation of the food you will display. I have outlined a number of different aspects of the processes, tools and preparation of yourself and the product you will be working with. Another part of this staging I would like to discuss before I show more examples of how to present the food, is the idea of atmosphere. Staging of your dishes can actually reach far beyond the plate itself. What I mean by this is you can consider things as far out from the food itself to the location on as wide a scale you may be able to provide. Let me explain it like this..**Staging can go from the plate or platter, to the table. Then from there to the room. From there, staging can go out to the area surrounding the room, meaning the house or building. Even further, staging can go from inside to outdoors. A park, or outside in a tent by a lake, even a in a parking lot.** All these can serve you well as different parts of the staging process, if you are thinking creatively. If you look at this **just like in chemistry as a formula, a staging equation** might look like this…

1. **Food items such as wings, hotdogs, burgers, corn on the cob etc.**
2. **Large decorative serving platters with garnish for the food**
3. **Theme oreintated serving ware, IE paper plates and cups with appropriate logo design**
4. **Large tables, like "dressed " picnic tables with benches and /or folding chairs**
5. **Outdoor location**
6. **Seasonal agreeability like late Summer, early Fall**

This is a perfect example of "**staging**" for **a holiday cookout**. Depending on the occasion, the possibilities are only limited by the budget and /or "stuff" you have to work with. **Take the same food items in number 1, replace 2 through 5 with foil pans, paper plates, the back of a pickup truck and a stadium parking lot during a football game and you will have tailgate party staging.** Now let's go back a few steps. You want to "stage" an elegant dinner at home for family or a few friends. If you only have **a plain table** to serve dinner on, you can make it much more suitable for elegance with a quick inexpensive trip to a dollar store. Get a **clean white tablecloth and a nice centerpiece for the table.** Even some **plastic plant in a nice glass vase** can be purchased to change the appearance of your meal completely. **This simple set up** is reminiscent of being in **a fine dining establishment** and will **compliment** your finished dishes.

You can **go from the table to the room** around where you will present you dishes so **use your imagination** and **set scenes. Paint the picture** of how you think it should look, using every resesource you have at your disposal. U'll be quite pleased what you can come up with when you practice "STAGING" with your whole heart and mind.

Chapter Four
" Carving"

As I explained earlier, in order to produce some food dishes that are works of art and not just something people will eat and forget all about your presentation you needed to have stuff to work with, tools etc. I also illustrated some tools for food carving. **Carving food** takes **a bit more skill** than just having stuff to work with and being a great cook. **Carving takes a lot of practice**. You can go to school or take classes to **learn how to carve food** or other items like **ice or clay** if you have the free time and budget to do so, and if you do, I would definetely suggest this course of action. **Carving can be a very complicated process that takes much patience** and as with any **skilled profession**, years of practice and at the least **some artistic skill**.

I didn't have the money or time to take classes so I taught myself by watching other carve and praticing on **cheap melons** whenever I had the oppurtunity to do so. I wanted to **add an extra dimension of art and beauty to the dishes I was presenting** since I already felt I had the way I wanted my recipes to look and taste already pretty much the way I felt they should be. With **carving skill** in your **cooking arsenal**, the possible ways **you can display presentations** is **almost endless**. You can **carve garnishes for dishes**, **sculptures to display with dishes** and even **scupltures of the food that will serve as dishes themselves** to present the food in. I have carved **melons, pumpkins, squash, apples, and oranges. Some fruit** give you the option to carve it entirely like melons because of **their solid structure** and **some, while soft inside** like an orange, are **best suited for the carving of their peel or outer skin.** You can **carve watermelons into baskets** that you can **serve the actual fruit inside.** People have asked me to **carve logos and names onto melons** to use as **centerpieces for their party tables.**

Carving can be a lot of fun and food items you carve will add another whole level of prestige and character to your finished dishes. Like I said, this part of food presentation takes some skill and practice to master, but even a novice or intermediate level carver can make some lovely dishes that will impress those you serve. Take a chance, give carving a try!

Chapter Five

"Color and Garnishing"

Color and garnishing is one of, if not THE most important aspect of artistic food presentation. Color shows vibration, freshness of the ingredients and continuity just like a picture in a frame. Too much of a certain color will not be pleasant to the eye and the unbalance of the dish will take away from its appeal, no matter how good it might taste. A perfect example of this might be a pasta dish flooded in red sauce so you can't even make out what kind of pasta it is. Some people love a lot of sauce and that's fine, just serve more of it on the side in a bowl.

Remember, **most people eat with their eyes first,** so a **lively colorful dish** will **get the juices going way before the dish is even touched.** **Nature** itself can play a big part in learning how to **put things together with colorful taste.** Just observe some different foods in their natural state, like **veggies or fruits fresh from the garden** or the **produce section of your supermarket.** Notice how the **watermelon is a lovely deep shade of red** inside when its cut open, and how **the black seeds accent this with their color and pattern.** It can be such a pleasing sight. Some people will bite the fruit, seeds and all, even if they spit them out after. Some people just swallow the bite, seeds and all,

Why? Because it looked that good, they didn't even have the desire to pick the seeds out, The whole thing looked good enough to eat and a lot of people will just go right into it every time and worry about the seeds later. Then it has the **dark green marbled outer skin, and bright whitish green inner rind bordering the red fruit** that almost makes it look surreal, like you wonder, WOW... how can **something just grow** and look like that **so naturally and beautiful**?

Without any help from **human hands** and **just a little earth and water, nature produces** some of the most **colorful and brilliant** pieces of **THE MOST HIGH** nourishment for us and the **colors** that show up **in nature are endless** and have been the **inspiration for artists** since painting and putting artistic expression on to paper or such fashionable mediums were first introduced to man..

I would like to mention **a food item from Japan** to elaborate more on how **color** and even **seasonal changes** can further be **used to visualize and express presentation.** The **Japanese** people make **a firm jelly like food** called, **Tokoroten.** It's produced by **sun drying high grade seaweed** and mixing it with the **purest spring water,** then **chilling it** until it becomes **a clear jelly.** It is used to make a **summer dessert** dish and is usually **cut into small squares.**

Due to its **clear appearance**, the cutting is done in this manner to give it **the look of ice cubes**, which when presented give the person eating it the **illusion of coolness**.

Garnishing is the art of using all those things you gather, ALL the "stuff" and the "staging" of useful items and colors, then put them together to highlight and enhance your final presentation. I've seen some people who are so good at garnishing their dishes, the way they make the dish look even outweighs the taste of the final product! And still, they get away with that because people are so overwhelmed by the way the food looks, they OVERLOOK the taste and all they talk about later is how lovely the presentation was. That is another reason why artistic food presentation is so important.

Some of the things I use to make **colorful garnishes** are just **leftover ends and cuts from other foods or the trimmings** from the preparation of the dish itself. **Herbs of all kinds** are always **perfect** to give **a fresh garden look and appeal to any platter.** I like to **throw fresh herbs like whole bunches of parsley into the deep fryer,** the results of which give turn the herbs into something that resembles **green plastic** and makes the **leaves super shiny and crispy,** which gives a totally **different look to the garnish. The herbs can still be eaten after they are fried** and even take on a **different flavor,** usually **stronger than if used fresh** but I do it just for the **appearance** of it.

Some **leafy green veggies such as spinach or kale** when **fried** turn **a richer, darker green** and can also be used to **enhance the look and taste quality** of your dish. **The stem top end of peppers and other veggies and fruits** make **lovely additions** to a **garnish.** I do a lot of **cutting boards** for the purpose of **carving whole cuts of meat in front of people. Garnishing the cutting boards** gives an **added attraction to people** standing and watching you carve. Also just seeing **the board beautifully designed** with the **meat sitting on it makes for a wonderful presentation** even if it is not being carved. You can simply **serve pre carved on a garnished board.** The list of **ingredients** and things you can use **to make a garnish is like art itself, endless.** I've made this book with more pictures than words because when it comes to **simple artistic food presentation,** I figure I can show you better than I can tell you!

Printed in the United States
By Bookmasters